Beams of Grief

Ludmila M. Flores

Beams of Grief

Ludmila M. Flores

ISBN (Print Edition): 978-1-54395-524-8

ISBN (eBook Edition): 978-1-54395-525-5

TABLE OF CONTENTS

PREFACE

I lost my husband after his twelve-year battle with cancer. It was February 28, 2018, at 5:44 a.m. Even today, I can still feel his last heartbeat in the palm of my right hand. When his heart took that last beat, the world did not tremble, the clock on the wall did not stop, an angel did not come, a beam of light did not brighten the room, no music fled the air…just a beat…silence…while the ignorant clock on the wall kept ticking, and the bird outside kept chiming, and the world kept moving forward. The world did not stop because I fought to remain standing in caregiver's shoes for fifteen years. The world did not end because my husband died.

During those fifteen years, my husband carried a heavy cross of both physical and mental illness. Twelve of those years he spent fighting stage IV cancer. I carried the cross with him while trying to keep our life as normal as possible, caring for all the "normal life problems" and the "normal challenges" of an emigrant family in the United States. We did it without extended family support; we—the Three Musketeers—went through this journey together: my husband, our cat, and I.

I do not know how I got to this point of my life. It was not an easy journey, and the cross grew heavier with every year that passed. My heart carries the scars of every single place we've been, every single moment we've managed, every single day we've survived. I've been a wife, caregiver, breadwinner. Now I am a widow. I am not sure how to handle it just yet.

For many years, my life was 99 percent focused on my husband—on everything that was going on in his life, everything he wanted to do, everything he did. My life was on hold. Then, within just a few days, I lost my husband, I moved out of our home, I donated all out possessions, I left school, our cat got adopted, I quit my job, and through the journey—as I realized later—I lost the girl inside of me.

I can't get my husband back, my cat is happy, I must figure out what the word "home" means to me, and I am painfully aware that the path

1

forward will not be possible without the girl who lost her way on the brutal hiking trial. So, let's start the journey: Step 1…

The first four months after my husband died, I wrote in a journal, which I called "Beams of Grief." It helped me survive. I hope you also find it helpful.

CHAPTER 1
WHEN THE SUN WENT DOWN IN THE MORNING

Though he'd been drinking liquids until about four hours ago, he's had nothing to eat for more than twenty-four hours. My husband is no longer able to swallow. His hands are warm and soft, but his feet are cool to the touch. His skin is turning a darker shade of color.

He talked to me before falling asleep into a deep, unresponsive slumber. I lie next to him, talking to him softly and calmly. Even though I receive no response, I'm hoping he can hear me. There is so much that needs to be said. It's hard to believe we saw each other every day for so many years. It seems there was not enough time to mention all the things I want to say now. I'm recounting favorite memories, places we visited, activities we shared. "I'm sorry for whatever I contributed to any stress or tensions or difficulties in our relationship," I say. "Helping you for twelve years through stage IV cancer, depression, anxiety, panic attacks, separation anxiety, and an array of other non-cancer-related health problems..." I trail off, then begin again. "...have not been easy. I tried so hard. I'm sorry for not trying harder." Tears roll down my cheeks. They are my only company.

He is restless and moves his arms and legs in repetitive motions. I quietly reassure him that the medicine he is getting in liquid form is nothing more than a pink and blue Italian Ice (Atavin and morphine) he is having while walking on the beach under the bright, golden sun. "Can you hear the waves crashing into the rocks?" To keep him comfortable, I apply glycerin on his lips—his favorite "Head to Toe" from Trader Joe's.

Periodically, I place a cold washcloth on his forehead to increase physical comfort. His breathing pattern is changing; it's slowing down and becoming shallow. I can hear a rattling sound. He stops breathing for five to thirty seconds at a time, and more medicine is coming. Again, I quietly reassure him that the medicine he is getting is nothing more than a pink and blue Italian Ice he is having while walking on the beach under the bright, golden sun. "Can you hear the ocean? It's calming down…moving back and forth…singing like a lullaby." I wonder if he can hear me or if I am talking to myself.

I talk to him and sing lullabies for twenty-four hours, practically nonstop. It's time to say good-bye and let him go. "I love you," I tell him. "Your father is waiting for you. Don't worry; you will be OK. I promise. Do not worry about me. You can let go. God is with us, and he will take care of both of us. It's okay to let go." I am lying in bed with him saying all that it is possible for me to say. I struggle for words. Every single one is an empty sound bouncing off the walls in the hospice room.

The nurse walks in and changes his position to make him more comfortable. More medicine is coming. And yet again, I quietly reassure him that the medication is nothing more than a pink and blue Italian Ice he is having while walking on the beach under the bright, golden sun. "Can you hear the ocean? Waves are singing songs about places faraway…all those places that we dreamed about but never went." I am holding his hand, and his breathing is slowing even more. "It's okay to let go. We both will be OK."

I am still holding his hand. The night is ending, and morning is slowly dancing in through the window. Birds begin serenading us. The clock on the wall is ticking. Birds and the clock are the only sounds I can hear. I feel peace. I could sit here holding my husband's hand and listening to the birds and clock forever.

I feel every beat of his heart in the right palm of my hand. Its calm steadiness is reassuring; it gives the impression that everything will be ok, that nothing bad will happen. We can do this. We have been through so much for so long. We've always managed. We've always made it through. We will beat this again, and he will be just fine. My confidence that all will be OK grows stronger. The next heartbeat seems stronger than the one before. I smile and take it as a sign that everything will be OK. It is 5:44 a.m., and his strong heartbeat has just confirmed life.

But another heartbeat does not come...I hear the birds sing outside of our window, and I hear the clock tick steadily in the room, but I do not feel his heart beat.

I wait for another pulse that does not happen. His heart has stopped. The heartbeat at 5:44 a.m. was not a sign of life but rather a good-bye.

CHAPTER 2
AT THE FUNERAL HOME

I asked to see him for the last time; all dressed up in his favorite suit, favorite tie, new white shirt, new shoes. I brought a box with things I wanted him to take with him: a picture, a letter, his favorite perfume, a tape of our wedding, and so on. His body was cold and stiff. He looked pale. He was not there; it was not him.

I took his hand, and it fit—it fit just right with mine. I was shocked, scared, and comforted all at the same time. I knew that hand so well. I knew that touch so well. I held his hand in mine, and it started getting warm and soft, bringing a surge of fear, confusion, and hope. "If I stand here long enough..." I thought. "If I keep holding his hand long enough, his heart might start beating again." I felt the responsibility and the need to just keep standing there holding his hand until I could feel that familiar heartbeat in the palm of my right hand.

Letting my husband's hand go was one of the hardest things I have ever done.

CHAPTER 3
KEEP GOING

Pick up dry cleaning, do laundry, clean, go shopping, plan dinner, drive to CVS, go to work, pay the bills, water the flowers, make lists in my head, fold the clothes, organize the drawer, clean the window, take the trash out, clean up the fridge, stop at the post office…so everything is ready and done when he comes home…Keep going like nothing has changed. Positive thinking…right…so things will be OK.

CHAPTER 4
ROSEWOOD BOX

The car smells like a wet dog. But the sky is the most beautiful color of blue. Looking at the world through the car window, I see trees, flowers, people, and sun shining through the branches and buildings; it's a perfect day. I feel like a cartoon in a bad Hollywood movie, sitting in the car with black, short boots; black pants; black top; and my hair down.

In my right hand, I'm holding a polished wooden box made from rosewood. The box is sheltered by a black velvet cover, and inside it are the ashes of my husband. Just three days ago, I held his hand. Just four days ago, I washed his face. Just six days ago, I spoon-fed him. And now the only thing I can touch is a wooden box full of dust.

Around me on the seat are birthday cakes. One looks like a train to wish my husband "A Good Journey." Another is shaped like an elephant to wish him "Good Luck." Birthday balloons are flying above me, pressing into the ceiling and dancing around my head with every bounce of the car. My husband died three days before his birthday, so I am throwing him a birthday party instead of a traditional ceremony. I wonder if he is going to attend the party. Maybe the door will open, and he will walk in.

How could a whole person fit into a rosewood box? Maybe the box of ashes is just a practical joke. Birthday balloons are dancing around my head; I'm holding cakes with my left hand and my husband's ashes with my right hand; I'm watching the world bathe itself in sunshine; and I'm doing all of this sitting in a car that smells like a wet dog. I'm breathing, and my heart is beating, but I am not sure if I'm alive.

CHAPTER 5
LAST GOOD-BYE

In my Last Good-Bye at the church, I attempted to summarize my husband's life in the space of five minutes. They were five very long minutes. Every single cell of my body echoed every word and every thought. I could not think about the funeral or the speech. The whole time I was contemplating that what I said right now, right here, could be the heroine speech that would bring my husband back. It happens that way, after all, in the movies.

I'm standing at the front of the church looking toward the back of the sanctuary, and I'm counting the steps between me and the outside door; I smell the air, noticing the light, examining every single inch between me and the door. The palms of my hands are ready to touch him, my legs are ready to run toward him, my arms are ready to hug him, my eyes are prepared to embrace him, and my lips are ready to kiss him.

My speech is almost done. I am dreading the last few words, the last letter echoing throughout the church. Silence. The church door remains closed. The distance between me and the door doubles in length somehow, and a few more seconds pass. My husband does not come back.

This is, in fact, my Last Good-Bye.

CHAPTER 6
THE WIFE

We were married for a very long time, but I never felt respected as "The Wife" by family and many around us. I have done so much as a caregiver: I have secured our life in a foreign country in every single way, and I have provided and secured the best health care available— all that without as little as a "job well done" The only time I was The Wife was during the couple of days following my husband's death. As The Wife, I planned the funeral and made all the decisions. As The Wife, I sat in the church while the priest served the Final Mass for my husband; the whole time he spoke directly to me—about my husband, about me, and about my husband and me. For the first time, everyone showed the respect that The Wife deserved. It's sad that it took my husband's death for me to finally get the respect and the recognition that should have been granted to me on the wedding day. Because I was always The Wife.

CHAPTER 7

KNOWING AND ACCEPTING

Knowing and accepting are two different things. After my husband's heart stopped, I waited for a few hours for it to start beating again. In the moment, I could not comprehend the "forever" aspect of the situation. I was convinced that if I sat next to him long enough holding his hand, his heart would start beating again.

For weeks, I did the logical things: I discussed with the medical team that my husband's cancer was spreading; I talked to the priest; I fought to get extra help; I spent hours talking to my health insurance provider; I started packing our apartment; I moved to hospice. But I never accepted any of it. None of the information or the events sank in. None of it registered on a deeper level. I was watching someone else's life.

I held my husband's hand for what seemed like eternity. But his heart did not start beating again. As his body started cooling down, his hand remained warm in mine.

Knowing and accepting are two different things.

CHAPTER 8
AUTOPILOT

I open the hospice door to the street, and I am immediately hit by a beam of sunshine. I cannot tolerate the bright light; I have been crying for hours and my eyes hurt. I'm closing my eyes and taking my first step. I'm entering the world without my husband, with my eyes closed.

Nothing makes sense. I feel disconnected, and I'm losing my ability to think logically. I can only feel, and my feelings do not make any sense; I cannot disassociate from the root of the situation. I cannot relate to my surrounding; the sun is brightly shining, the sky has the most beautiful blue color, I can smell fragrant flowers in the air, and the whole world seems wrapped up in a blanket of peace while I feel completely lost and displaced.

I am moving forward like a robot, making all the necessary phone calls and taking all the required steps. A part of me cannot be reached; it is stuck some place inside of me—heavy, lost, and lonely. That part of me is not able to connect with people, experiences, surroundings, thoughts, memories…not even the blue sky and sunshine. I am operating in autopilot mode.

CHAPTER 9
MR. ALONE

My husband died twenty-four hours ago after twelve long years with stage IV cancer and fifteen years total of various health issues; his medical record is a mile long. Somehow there was always just me and him…or just me… sitting alone in the waiting room, sitting alone at his bed site, standing alone in the emergency room, talking alone to the medical team, walking alone back and forth in the hospital hall, taking care of him alone yet another night, alone yet another day with "Mr. Alone." He was with me for fifteen years. He was good company for me. Are we going to remain friends? I kind of hope we stay friends. Mr. Alone gave me more support than all the family combined.

CHAPTER 10

BARE

I have suddenly been stripped bare of everything; I am naked from head to toe, from my heart to my soul. All my vital functions have stopped, but somehow, I am still alive. Still breathing, still feeling, still hearing my beating heart, aware of the pain I am feeling. Other than that, I am numb and cold.

It's a crisp, early, spring morning, and I am standing on the top of a cliff. My bare hands are stretching to the sky, and I am trying to hold on to the clouds. But they are slipping through my fingers. I am the missing link between the earth and the sky. With my bare feet, I am trying to stand on a slippery stone; with my naked body I am trying to stand straight and still, so I keep standing just a little longer before falling down the cliff.

I can see far into the horizon—the whole world at my feet. The sun is rising, and everything seems at peace, beautiful, and full of life. The dewdrops are falling on my face and mixing with my tears. With my bare hands, I am trying desperately to hold on to the fluffy white clouds, but I am growing weaker. I am trying frantically to stand still and stand strong, but I do not have any strength left, and my fingers can't reach the clouds. I am falling down the cliff.

CHAPTER 11

THE GUILD

I can name a million mistakes I have made, a million shortcomings I have, a million things I could have done better, a million sentences I could have spoken more wisely, a million words that could have been more appropriate, a million moments I could have made more bearable, a million situations in which I could have been stronger, a million times I wish I had been less tired, a million seconds I wish I had smiled more, a million favors I could have fulfilled for my husband, a million disappointments I could have avoided, a million worries I could have made worry-free, a million nights I could have made more memorable, a million evenings I could have wished upon a star, a million somethings I could have done a million times better. The guild is so overpowering, I cannot breathe. I am paralyzed.

I am looking at my husband's cane and thinking to myself that the cane never failed my husband the way I did. The cane provided support day and night, strong and steady, never tired, never upset, and never wrong. I am looking at my husband's pillow and thinking that the pillow was always there for him, day and night, soft and supportive. I am looking at the blanket and thinking that the blanket was always there for him day and night, sweet and comforting.

Only I, I have failed him.

CHAPTER 12
POLITICALLY CORRECT

I am tired of being politically correct: Why didn't you tell us more about this? You must do this. You must do that. Why didn't you call us and tell us that? Why didn't you communicate better? Why didn't you follow up the protocol? Why you are making decision A? Why aren't you making decision B? You should have done this. You should have done that!

Stop! Please stop!

I am in my pain. I do not know how to get up from the bed in the morning.

Is anyone worried about me?

Anyone?

CHAPTER 13
LIFE SENTENCE

Today, they asked me to fill out a legal form; they asked me to put my husband in a box titled "Prior Husband." I stared at it for ten minutes unable to comprehend why I couldn't place his name in the box titled "Current Husband." I argued with the clerk for thirty minutes, then tossed the form to the trash and stormed out of the building. I was so angry! How stupid is that? What she meant: "He is no longer your husband." Then it hit me. I finally realized…He can't be my "Current Husband"; I am a widow. Widows do not have a "Current Husband". No matter what I do in my life, I will always be a widow.

I am a widow for life.

CHAPTER 14
GIVE ME A BREAK!

I was taught to approach life with logic and reason. Logic and reason—I have tried to do my best to do just that all my life until now. Now, life does not make sense. What is the logic and reason in my husband's death? What it the logic and reason of losing my husband so early in life? What was the point of watching my life pass by for fifteen years? I do not see one!

I have been asked and advised to trust in God. I have been told that God has a plan for me. I understand he is God. However, I do not know how to trust him. I do not know how to follow him. I do not follow his plan. I do not know his plan. Moreover, frankly so far, I am not too fond of his idea for my life. Yes, I know my liking or understanding is irrelevant to God, but it is relevant to me, and I do not know how to live a life feeling like I am trapped in a spider's web. Yes, all I am feeling, someone already felt before me. And someone else is feeling it right now. Probably, despite everything, that person is following God without questions and tantrums. However, I am me, not someone else. I am I. So, give me a break everyone. God included!

I am sorry for being so rude. No, I am not sorry at all. Being rude is feeling quite good right now. I am hurting too much to be polite. I am hurting so much and on so many different levels that I do not think I have inside of me a pain-free inch. I want to jump out of my body and just run and run some place pain-free and tears-free. I am hurting in so many places and so many ways. I want someone to wrap hands around me and help me through the day. Just hold me and say nothing. I do not feel like trusting or listening to anyone right now, God included! Moreover, you know what, God? If you are reading this, you made me, you know me, you know everything…thus, you need to understand that I am acting out. You need to be patient, and I must survive yet another moment in time. Until then, give me a break! All of you. God included!

CHAPTER 15
A MESSAGE

There is so much I want to tell you. There is so much I want to say…
But you are not here. So, I walk around writing your name on everything
that I find in my way. I write "I love you" on little flat stones. I write your
name and "I miss" you in the sand, dirt, leaves, and in the air. I hope you
see my message. I hope you get my message. I hope you know what I am
trying to say. If you do, I hope that one day you will write me back and say,
"Hi there, don't you see my footprints in the sand next to yours?"

CHAPTER 16
SMASHED GLASS

I have learned that if you are angry and you crash a glass against the wall, the following happens:

It does not have the same WOW effect and momentum as it does in the movies. You know what I am talking about. That moment when a glass flies through the air and then hits the wall in slow motion, cracks, breaks, and flies away in little pieces. You and the rest of the theater hold your breath while watching the whole thing sitting in comfortable chairs, eating popcorn, and drinking soda. You hold your breath watching the glass hit the wall, and you go…Oooh! Breathe!

Real life is not like that at all:

- There is no small motion in the act of breaking a glass against the wall. Before you realize you did it, it's done. Before you fully comprehend the whole "I am angry, I am taking a glass into my hand, I am throwing the glass against the wall," it's done! No wow! No Oooh! No momentum! No small motion!

- It does not have the same effect…an angel does not show up at your door just because you are angry and you smashed a glass against the wall.

- You are not going to have that big Hollywood I-am-angry moment on a big screen.

- You are alone, so no one is going to notice. No one is going to know you are angry. Perhaps throwing the glass with an audience around might help.

- At some point, you need to calm down and clean up the mess. You see, what they do not tell you in the movies is that the glass truly breaks into a gazillion million pieces. In the movies,

they do not tell you that you will spend the next month finding these pieces in the most improbable places all over your
home, even in areas where you did not break anything.

- I can assure you that at least a third of these gazillion million pieces will find a way to pierce your skin
  at some point during the month and beyond.

- Smashed glass changes nothing. Nothing at all. Nothing.

- Broken glass relives your anger for about 0.000001 second.

- Smashed glass does nothing to ease your pain.

In conclusion, smashing glass against a wall looks great on the big
screen when the camera zooms on the rotating glass hurling through the
air, the crack after crack of disintegrating glass, the flying pieces; and the
sound person enhances the sound, the special effects person enhances the
flying trajectory of a few pieces, and the lights person plays with the dancing light and reflection…

However, smashing an ordinary glass against an ordinary wall in
ordinary light in the regular apartment of an ordinary girl in the midst
of everyday life only creates an ordinary mess that the average girl will be
cleaning for the next ordinary month.

Smashed glass changes nothing. Nothing at all. Nothing!

CHAPTER 17
STRONG ME

My husband always said, "It's just you and me." Then he was suddenly gone. I must say it is scary and lonely to be just me. People around me keep telling me I am one of the strongest and most resilient people they have ever met. Today alone, I heard these statements at least a dozen times—from a nurse, a friend, others. I am not sure how they reached such a conclusion. They know perhaps 30 percent of what I have been through. If they knew it all, what would they say about me? What would that make me? A superhero? A superwoman? Many also told me that I am not alone because I have my strong self. I am not sure what that means:

- I have my strong self to talk to my strong
  self when my strong self is down.

- I have my strong self to hold my hand and
  run fingers through my hair.

- I have my strong self to give my strong self a hug.

CHAPTER 18
DECISIONS

I have made so many decisions, resolutions, and plans since my husband died. One day I write them down, and the next day I burn the list in the candle flame.

CHAPTER 19
BLACK HOLE

There is a black hole in my brain and a heavy fog. I am not sure who I am anymore. I am no longer a wife. I cannot focus, I cannot remember, I cannot think. My husband died ten days ago, and I am frightened that I am already forgetting him and the life we had together. I am walking back and forth from one corner of a room to another trying to get ahold of myself. I cannot remember anything. It feels like someone just took a big eraser and erased our life together. The problem is that the woman staring at me from the mirror does not look like I did before everything…when I was just a twenty-year-old girl. She is an adult woman, and her pain is so thick you can touch it.

I am standing in the middle of a dark tunnel unable to recall places we lived in and things we did together. I feel unbearable pain. I am hurting so badly that I am about to faint. Sometimes when the pain comes, I cannot get off the floor. Each glimpse of our life together feels like I am stabbing myself with a knife and turning the blade slowly inside me.

Perhaps it is better not to remember. But then the panic and fear set in from not remembering. There is a black hole in my brain and a heavy fog. I am not sure who I am anymore. I cannot focus, I cannot remember, I cannot think. I am frightened that I am already forgetting my husband and the life we had together.

CHAPTER 20
BREATHE

I have only one word to say:
Breathe!

CHAPTER 21
JUST GO FOR IT

People keep telling me, "You do not get anything unless you ask for it." Books and audiotapes encourage me to send out positive energy, and they ask, "What are you willing to give up for the things you want?" I do not know. Can I ask for my husband back? Can I ask for my fifteen years back? What should a wife offer in return for the life of her husband? What should a person offer to get back fifteen years of life? Anyone...?

CHAPTER 22
FIX

Stop fixing other people's problems. Stop worrying about everyone around you for once in your life. Stop being the one who puts everyone around you first, before yourself. Fix your problem; worry about your own broken heart.

That is enough to do for one human.

CHAPTER 23
HOME

Sometimes home is among people you have never seen, never lived with, never talked to. Hospice was my home for a little while. Home is where they care for you, ask if you are OK. No one from my family asked me if I am OK, but the hospice nurse did several times a day.

CHAPTER 24
LIKE NOTHING HAPPENED!

My husband died two weeks ago. A big piece of the world is missing, and this ridiculously ignorant and oblivious crowd around me acts as if nothing has happened, nothing has changed. Nothing at all, moving on! The world is fine! Everything is just great!

I am putting one foot in front of the other, walking through the crowd. The crowd is annoying and frustrating. I want to get out of it! I want to get through it! I want to get to a more comfortable space! Unfortunately, today the crowd is even more annoying and frustrating than any other day. People are stepping on my toes, whacking me with their backs as they pass around me, hitting me with their elbows…not even acknowledging that they are causing a problem. I feel invisible! I feel misplaced! I feel alone! I want to scream! I am in so much pain I do not think I can take another step. No one cares!

I am like a clock that lost one of its arms and half of its wheels, and instead of tick-tock-tick-tock, I am just doing tick-heartbeat-tick-silence. The ticking sound resonates through the crowded street; my heartbeat is getting louder. No one hears me, no one sees me, no one shares my pain. I am standing on the sidewalk, and I do not understand how the world can keep turning, how everyone keeps going about their business when my husband is not here anymore and my heart is broken. I want to scream, "How can you keep walking, shopping, talking? Don't you know that my husband died, my husband is not here, my husband is gone?!" Instead, I just stand in the middle of the sidewalk. No one cares!

CHAPTER 25
UNIVERSE EMERGENCY UNIT

People always told me that by the age of forty you should know what you want from life and where you stand in life…or else! Or else there is something wrong with you and you need to call the "Universe Emergency Unit" to save you. It is now or never!

People always told me that by the age of forty you should have a husband, house, children, education, car, at least one vacation a year, and so on. People always told me how I should live and when.

So, I am desperately waiting for the Universe Emergency Unit (UEU) to rescue me and set me on the correct path. But the UEU is not showing up. Hi People, is there a number I can call? Is there a fax number I can fax a formal request to be rescued? An email perhaps? Anyone?

CHAPTER 26
THE ROUTINE

I lost my husband three weeks ago, and everyone is telling me I must go back to my routine. I tried! Honestly, I tried! But this has been my routine:

I wake up in the morning, wash up, dress, prepare medicine and breakfast for my husband. I make lunch for my husband before going to work. I work and periodically call home to check up on my husband. He is feeling pain in his back today; he might need more medicine. During lunch break, I made a list of what I need to buy for my husband: pharmacy, CVS, specialty pharmacy, dry cleaning, groceries…Before leaving work, I check emails for information related to my husband's health; I check the latest medical news about his condition. On my way home, I stop to pick up my husband's medicine, and I get his shower gel in CVS—the one he likes from Johnson & Johnson because his skin is sensitive from the cancer treatment. Then I stop at Trader Joe's and get groceries. Do not forget the red beets, sweet potatoes, fish, and beer; his GI issues have improved and maybe he can enjoy a sip. I walk back home, and at the door, my husband is reporting that he is hungry. I'm glad he has an appetite. Before taking my coat off, I walk to the kitchen and take food out of the freezer. Then I take advantage of the fact that my husband is on the balcony, so I start the laundry; my husband is not very fond if its sound. Finally, I take my coat off and quickly swipe the dirt from the floor before he slips on it and hurts himself. I give fresh water and food to our cat. OK, time for a quick shower and back to the kitchen to prepare my husband's dinner and perhaps start lunch for tomorrow. I can bake the potato for tomorrow, and fish and salad can be done fresh in the morning before I leave for work. During dinner, my husband and I recap his day—the work, the students (he teaches piano), of course his health problems, his medicine, his doctor's emails. Looks like new side effects are popping up, so let's see if we can handle them by ourselves; let's try a few things before calling the medical team. Yes, I can contact the nurse, but "it would be better if you call because you are the patient." The laundry is drying. Good. I quickly check today's mail: trash… trash…bill…bill…Have to check the balance in our bank account. Must call to check the phone bill; I will pay in the morning or during my lunch break and drop it off on my way home. I must call the health insurance and check on our green card status—two things that always stress me because my husband's life and treatment depend on my ability to secure our legal status in the United States and to provide health insurance for him. I must buy more fresh vegetables and eggs. My husband is searching for a nice movie to watch. OK, I'll wash the dishes quickly, and the potato for tomorrow can be turned off. I suppose we can watch a video tonight since my husband had a good day; sometimes we watch just the news if it is too late or he is not doing too well. He is often very tired. He is an amazing piano teacher, but to shine and excel during his piano lessons, he needs to give all he has…and it is time to go to sleep…one more recap how he did in the bathroom…medication…hope you sleep well…sweet dreams. Hopefully my husband will have depression and pain free nigh. Good night.

I lost my husband three weeks ago, and everyone is telling me I must go back to my routine. I tried! I did! I woke up in the morning, washed up, dressed, went to work, worked, walked back home, took my coat off, showered, and went to sleep. Good night!

CHAPTER 27
HEY, YOU!

Hey, you! People! Stop telling me what to do. Stop telling me when to wake up, when to go to sleep, what to wear, how to brush my hair; that I should cut my hair, change my makeup, go for a trip, take a vacation, take a break, do not take a break, date, do not date, have dinner, go to a concert, go dancing, work, don't work…There is a difference in telling me what to do and suggesting what to do.

Hey, you! People! When I am ready, I will book a flight to the North Pole or to the planet Mars. For now, let me sit on the beach and cry.

CHAPTER 28
THE NIGHT

I love the night. The stars above my head. Looking for the moon shining down and showing me the path, saying hello from space. Telling us there is something bigger than dying.

CHAPTER 29
THERE YOU GO

Just one goal today. Place one foot in front of the other and keep moving forward. Right foot, left foot, right foot, left foot…one step, two steps, three steps, four steps…just keep moving forward!

CHAPTER 30
FALLING OFF A CLIFF

I am falling off a cliff. I grew up from a child into a woman next to my husband. I have two graduate degrees, I have a job, I secured legal status in the United States for both of us, I know how to take care of myself, I know how to take care of a husband, and I know how to take care of a home. But I have never been an adult without my husband. It feels like falling off a cliff.

I am falling off a cliff. Who's got my back? Only me! No one is waiting at home for me. No one will know if I get sick during the night. No one will know if I do not come home at night. No one will buy flowers for my birthday. No one will wipe tears off my face. No one will hold my hand. No one will stroke my face. No one will touch my hair. No one will call me by my nickname. No one will watch me in my sleep. No one will…I am falling off a cliff.

Counseling, friends, family…everyone is on a different schedule from mine, and they have a million other things to do besides talking to me. Loneliness makes my problems feel bigger and my situation worse. I want to tell you all that I appreciate your help, but please give me time and space. Phrases such as "Time heals all wounds," "God never gives you more than you can carry," "You need to move on," "He would want you to be happy," …Stop! Just stop. I need to figure things out on my own. I cannot move on when I am not able to stand up. I cannot start to heal if I am not even sure how big my wound is. I cannot lean on God if I do not understand what he wants from me! Be patient with me. I am falling off a cliff!

CHAPTER 31
DEAL WITH IT

My heart is still beating, and I am still breathing…whether I like it or not…whether I feel like it or not. The fact is, I am breathing, and my heart is beating.

Deal with it!!!

CHAPTER 32
I AM A COOKIE

Someone just told me, "Do not worry. You will survive. You will come out of this much stronger than you are now. You are unbreakable." One day, at some point, I will survive, and I will be stronger. Because deep down I have such a hunger for life, and in some place in my heart, there is a list—a mile-long list—of things I must do before I die.

I am unbreakable, but right now, I am breaking inside. I am a chocolate chip cookie that someone forgot in the cookie jar. The cookie is lonely, sitting quietly inside its confines, and it is starting to crumble. There is a strange peace within the cookie jar—quiet and heavy, disturbed only by the cookie's occasional cry. Every tear and every whisper bounce off the jar's insides like a rubber ball off a wall, making the sound go on forever. I am a cookie, and I am crumbling apart.

CHAPTER 33
MEDICINE

I found medicine for pain that costs nothing. But you need to leave the door to your heart wide open: songs, movies, pictures, jokes, sunsets, flowers.... They do not provide a cure, but they suppress the symptoms.

Sometimes movies can be very healing. They let you cry for others, be angry at others, smile with others, worry about the problems of others. And that is sometimes easier than facing your own reality. Movies let you feel the pain of other people or no pain at all for a moment; they let you worry about someone else's problems or not worry at all just for a second.

Pictures, songs, and your surroundings can be very healing. Do you feel pain watching the sunrise? Do you feel pain when the sun says its first hello in the morning crossing the horizon? Do you have pain watching the world bathe in an explosion of bright colors under the shadow of vanishing night? Do you have pain when the tones of your favorite songs wrap around you and let you dream?

I found medicine for pain that costs nothing. But you need to leave the door to your heart wide open.

CHAPTER 34
HIDING

Forty-eight hours of hiding. Hiding under the cover watching TV series with an endless number of episodes about whatever…and doing nothing else…and that is OK.

CHAPTER 35
I WANT TO STOP FALLING

I need to stop falling. I've been falling off the cliff for so long that I can't feel my body or my soul. I have plunged into ice-cold water, and I am numb. The downward movement of my little me does not seem to be following the Earth's gravity. If it were, I would have hit the ground a long time ago. Instead, my downward movement seems to cycle, goes on and off gravity, and I am falling, bouncing, floating in the air, falling. Every single cell in my body is numb, and I am out of breath. I do not have the energy to do this anymore.

I need to stop falling. I do not care how much it will hurt when I finally hit the ground. I need to stop falling. I want to hit bottom. I want to crash down, and I do not care if I hit a pillow or a rock. I want to stop falling. I am ready to hit the ground, and I do not care if I die or survive. I can't keep falling any longer.

CHAPTER 36
THE SIGN

I am waiting for "The Sign." My husband died six weeks ago, and all I feel is emptiness. I remember his energy, his smile, his warmth, his spirit, his touch, his fears, his pain, his anger, his confusion, his sorrows, his last heartbeat. How could all that disappear? How can all that be gone? The hole left in me and around me feels wider and deeper than the universe. I worry I might disappear in it.

Every day I look for The Sign. You know, like in the movies. The Sign assures you that everything is OK: a butterfly flies where no butterfly ever lived before and sits on the palm of your hand; the car that doesn't even have a motor suddenly starts its engine; the death rose suddenly grows overnight and blooms with the most beautiful flowers...The Sign! The unmistakable Sign that you cannot ignore even if you try. The Sign that you know is real even if you tell yourself a million times over that signs do not exist, that you do not believe in them.

I have been looking for The Sign since my husband died. I have not found it yet. I see familiar things. I remember moments. Small things are happening. However, I have not seen The Sign that tells me my husband is OK, I am OK, we are OK, the world is OK. I am waiting for The Sign. Where is it? Anyone?

CHAPTER 37
HUMAN

I am faced with the painful reality of being just a simple, unperfect human. However, God made me a human for a reason…I suppose…perhaps. If God would like me to be God, I guess he would not have made me human. I am just a human.

CHAPTER 38
MY GRIEF

People are dying every day, so why is my grief special? Because it is MY grief and the biggest thing happening in MY life. Grief does not come in steps, levels, or stages. For me, grief is a nonlinear entity. It comes, stays, and goes, returns, changes in a different form...It is a roller-coaster ride, and I never know when I am heading up and when I am heading down, or when I am just standing still. I never know when it is going to hit me the hardest.

I want to "lose it" for once—throw things on the ground, scream, yell. I would like to just quit everything, set something on fire, stop paying the bills, be irresponsible, be carless, be carefree...however, instead I continue to be politically correct, polite, kind, and helpful. And that is not helpful to me.

It is MY husband who died, and the fifteen years of MY life that feel lost. I was not holding the hand of the others who died I did not kiss their lips, I did not share a smile with them, I did not wipe their tears, I did not care for their pain, I did not walk with them on the beach and say, "I love you. Let's dream."

People are dying every day, so why is my grief special? Because it is MY grief and the biggest thing happening in MY life. I do not care if others come home. I need my husband to walk through the door and say, "I love you, and I am home." I need my fifteen years back right now.

CHAPTER 39
I AM LUCKY

Watching the raindrops and the dark clouds moving in, I feel sorry for people suffering from the blues and seasonal depression as my husband did among many other challenges. I am finding quite a comfort in the darkness of the clouds; it is like pulling a blanket over my body, letting the pain hide in the shadow of the clouds for a little while. The raindrops are touching the palm of my hand, kiss after kiss.

Clouds are giving the sun a break and some privacy. We all need our time off—even the sun. The clouds are curtains closing the sunshine show then saying, "I hope to see you back soon. I hope you had fun with people down there. Now go home to your family in the sky." I feel so blessed and so grateful to be alive enjoying the rain and the darkness of clouds; I wish everyone with the Winter Blues would get at least a little bit of the feeling that heals my heart at this moment.

CHAPTER 40
DUCT TYPE

I never knew the human heart could feel so much pain. I am afraid that at any moment my chest will burst, and my heart will explode. A human heart can't bear so much pain! My heart can't bear so much pain. Sometimes I feel I cannot take it anymore. The pain is so strong and unbearable. I can't breathe. I am paralyzed. I can't stand straight.

Then, I smile; my last "reasonable and logically thinking" brain cell has recalled a cartoon: "Everything can be fixed with duct tape." Maybe I can wrap duct tape around my heart…miles and miles of duct tape nice and tight so my heart does not explode. Perhaps that will keep my heart beating a little longer.

Sometimes, I tell my heart to keep beating. Sometimes, I ask it to stop. Sometimes, I wish it finally would break and stop beating because I cannot take the pain anymore. I'm waiting for my heart to give up. Every morning I'm surprised to wake up with a beating heart in my chest. Every evening I'm amazed that my heart managed to survive another day. Sometimes, I think my heart has only minutes to live. The pain is escalating…and then…like a switch, it stops for just a millisecond when I see a bird, a squirrel, a funny cloud, a beautiful flower, or I hear a song…somehow my heart does not need much to feel better. I never knew the human heart could be so resilient.

"Hi, you! Heart, you better keep beating!" It is incredible what a millisecond of beauty, fun, or a smile can do for a hurting heart. However, I wonder…In case my heart stops tomorrow, how do I want to spend my last day?

Dancing in the moonlight with wildflowers in my hair.

CHAPTER 41
NO ONE ASKED ME

What the hell is this? Sitting on the park bench, gazing over the green grass, beautiful trees, and birds cheerfully jumping around. What the hell is this? A breathtaking blue sky above my head, clouds asking my fingers to touch them, sun so gentle in the morning hours that I want to snuggle closer to it. What the hell is this? In the middle of all that innocent, fragile, and vulnerable beauty, there is me. What the heck is this? What type of reality show? No one asked if I want to be on it! I was just added as an extra, and somehow, I have become the leading lady on a show in which I did not want to participate in the first place. What the hell is this?

THE OCEAN

"Can the ocean heal everything?" I feel so small standing in the middle of the beach—stiff, paralyzed with pain, barefoot, waist-long hair blowing in the wind…anything but free. I walk through the shallow water of the endless ocean. The numbing effect of the ice-cold salt water on my feet travels directly to my broken heart, and at least for that short moment, I feel my heart is numb enough to beat again pain-free. The sound of outer ocean on the beach is so loud that I can scream and cry and hear my voice disappearing in the endless waves. The sound of wind above the sea understands my pain, and with a kind understanding, it carries my words without judgment.

"Can the ocean heal everything?" It lifts my anxiety and brings calm. Sitting in silence at the shore, watching the waves washing my pain away, hearing the surf. For the time I am here, I am hurting less, and my heart can take a beat. How long can I stay? Thirty minutes, one hour, four hours? I take ten minutes. The missing inside me feels smaller, and the pain is a little bit more bearable against the big, vast ocean without end. Waves carry my problems into the horizon, far away from me. I close my eyes, smelling the salty air, letting the wind dry my tears and cool my cheeks. And then I rest in the sand. I am not sure if the ocean can heal everything, but it allows my heart to take a beat…almost pain-free.

CHAPTER 43
THE SUPERMARKET

I have browsed the supermarket for almost an hour. My shopping cart is full. I've read all the labels at least twice. I'm happy I found everything on my list, the list in my head. I am planning dinner, and as I approach the cashier, cold air wraps around my body; I feel sick, and I can't breathe. I look at my clenched fists. I feel lightheaded, and I glance over my shopping cart, realizing for the first time that I have just picked all my husband's favorite foods and practically nothing that I would want to eat. I leave the shopping cart two feet from the cashier, and in zombie-like mode, I walk out of the store. Breathe…look at the sky…breathe…I do not want to shop ever again.

Breathe…

CHAPTER 44
A FRIEND

I am blessed with a very few people who are helping me on my journey through grief. However, I am shocked by all the so-called friends who are interested only in the gain from someone's hardship and pain. Anything that they can get from free stuff to free labor from you is a fair game. So, they say.

Who is a friend? A friend is someone who tells you to go for a walk. A friend is someone who tries to understand you and does not judge! A friend is someone who hugs you and helps you think, cry, talk, or stay still without saying anything at all. A friend is someone who gives you space and leaves you alone. A friend is someone who offers home with no strings attached. A friend is someone who smiles when you smile. A friend is someone who lights up a fire for you. A friend is someone who tells you to watch the sun go down over the water.

A friend loves you unconditionally, and friendship is free!

CHAPTER 45
THE DOOR IS CLOSED

The door to my past is closed. A big lock is hanging on it, and the only thing I can do is watch my life from outside through the window like an uninvited guest. I am shattered as I've never been before. The big lock is a painful reminder that my past is gone. I see my life flashing in the window glass. I am scared to turn my back to my past. Because of tears, I do not see today. Because of pain, I cannot imagine the future.

WHERE ARE YOU, GOD?

Where are you, God, when I need you? I have not always believed in you. I have questioned you many times. But you know I've tried. Yes, I've failed many times. Life has driven me to my knees more than once. I am afraid I will never get back up all by myself and be me again. So, I beg you to help me. I'm sorry for everything I've done wrong; I'm sorry for my doubts, I'm sorry for not listening. I can't promise you to be great from now on, but I promise I will try. I will keep trying to be better every day.

My husband always said, "Trust God." Even when I did not believe, even when I was not listening, even when I did not trust. He said, "Trust God. His is all we have. We are nothing without him." And yes, if you do not have the same strength and unshakable fight as my husband did (I know I do not), you will find yourself shouting at God and the whole world, crying yourself to sleep, hiding in the corner of your room in despair, demanding to know what the heck is going on! What is the point of going through something this hard and this horrible for fifteen years and at the end finding yourself in the box called "A Widow"?!

Where are you, God, when I need you? I did not always believe in you. I have questioned you many times. However, you know I have tried. Are you walking next to me? I cannot feel you. I cannot see you. I cannot hear you. I see only one set of footprints in the sand,

and I hope they are yours, because I can barely stand.

CHAPTER 47
PEOPLE!

People! Please stop confusing symptoms with the problem. My problem is not that I have depression or post-traumatic stress. I do not have a disease called "depression." The disease, the cause, is the loss of my husband, the loss of time. I can't eliminate the cause. I can't treat the cause. I must learn how to live with it the same way people learn how to live with a chronic illness. There is no cure. There is no point-of-return.

People! I am not infectious. Do not cross the street to the other side so you don't have to talk to me. If you do, cross it well so it's not so apparent you are avoiding me. I am hurting, but I am not contagious. If you do not want to talk to me, just say hello and keep walking.

People! If you don't want to offer help, don't! I never asked you for anything! Do not feel obligated to help! I don't care for your help! Just say, "Have a great day." Please do not go on and on about how you will always be there for me. If you care about me at all, send me a funny picture, a song, recommend a movie to me, send me a flower, a smile. You do not have to care for me! I was independent before my husband died, I am independent now, and I will be independent in the future.

People!

CHAPTER 48
CLARITY

The brain fog is gone, and my memory is better than ever. Unfortunately. Fortunately. Take a chance and speak up. Open another door, ask for another story from my past. I know; it will be even more painful than the first and more heartbreaking than the next. But Mr. Brain is back! He remembers everything. He is ready for anything. World, here we come!

PERHAPS

It was the worst night yet. I knew I could not survive it, would not escape it. Then suddenly I felt his hand on my forehead and a stream of energy, calmness, and peace. I stopped spiraling down. I just knew it was Him. He stayed until I fell asleep. He was gone in the morning.

Perhaps my husband came back to help me through the night. Maybe God sent him to help me one more time. Perhaps it was an angel. Maybe it was God. Perhaps my brain played a trick on me. Maybe my neurons just fired up in despair. But I survived the worst night yet.

Believe what you want. Think what you wish. It does not matter what you call it. It does not matter what you believe in. Thank you for my husband. Thank you for my angel. Thank you for my brain. Thank you for my imagination. Thank you for my neurons. Thank you, God, for you.

…. I know it was You…

CHAPTER 50
HEART VS. BRAIN

My heart is in constant disagreement with my brain. My brain is in constant dispute with my heart. My heart is broken but has so much feeling and energy to live. My mind is on strike, pretty much refusing to accept the reality. Before and immediately after my husband's death, it was the opposite—my brain knew but my heart refused to accept it. Now, it is the other way around. I suppose I am lucky that the rest of my body does not have a mind of its own.

CHAPTER 51
LIFE IS NOT DONE WITH ME

For a long time, it is going to be just you, grief, and pain. After that, it will be you, the sorrow, the pain, and the next chapter of your life. Learn who can you trust, who you can truly believe. I must learn to trust myself. I am learning to carry my head high. I can't decide that I am done with life, because life never listens to me and I have the feeling that life is not done with me. So, let's keep the head up, keep breathing, and following something to touch and feel. Sorry to tell you, girl in the mirror, no one is going to be there for you and life is not done with you just yet.

CHAPTER 52
HAPPY

People keep telling me to focus on being happy. What is being happy? Happy is:

the wind in my long hair

the raindrops that soak me wet

the song in my head

the music that makes me dance

the picture that makes me smile

the touch that says, "I care"

the wildflower in my hair

the hug that makes me feel safe

the good book in my hand

the walk in the middle of a carless road

the wind kissing my cheeks

the sand under my feet

the soft pillow that snuggles in my arms before I go to sleep

the fragrance of the pine tree

the rose-petal bubble bath

the train that goes far

the water that reflects light

the campfire at night

the music that tree leaves sing

the tingle in my eyes when I dream.

CHAPTER 53
THE FIRST DAY

The first day of the rest of my life...How do you embark on the future when your past gone? It's like building the roof on a house and at the same time taking the foundation apart. "Just have courage," the universe says. What happen if you do not? How much courage do you need? A mountain or a speck? A week of courage or a second of courage? I suppose the amount or size is irrelevant. If you can find courage, you are good to go!

The first day of the rest of my life...Everything seems frightening. I am like a little girl the first day of school. I am walking on thin ice; one wrong step and I will disappear into the freezing water. I hold my breath just a little with every step I make. I presume it would not be scary if it would not be essential for my journey forward.

So here we go! Step one.

CHAPTER 54
I WANT YOU TO KNOW

I want you to know that you are not alone even though most of the time you might feel like you have been left on planet Mars with only one tank of oxygen, a torn suit, cracked helmet, no water, no food, no shelter, and no other humans to talk to. I was sure I would not survive the fifteen-year journey as a caregiver, or the end of the journey. Somehow, I survived both. I am not sure how or why.

Whatever you are feeling is normal. Even though that phrase "All you are feeling is normal" makes me angry even today. Perhaps because I tend to associate "normal" feelings with something positive. Feelings like "I am falling from a cliff," "I just want to put on the brake and stop the world from moving forward," "I want to take a fragile object and smash it against the wall," "I want to scream at the world and kill…something…perhaps my pillow"—these feelings are somewhat out of my comfort zone.

Nevertheless, whatever you are feeling is normal. We all grieve differently. Do not let anyone tell you how you should be mourning or how long you should be grieving or what you should do or how you should do it. If people's suggestions and advice make you uncomfortable or upset, turn around and walk away. There is no reason to let people make you feel worse than you are already feeling. No apology necessary.

I have found myself grieving because of the fifteen-year journey and grieving because of the way it all ended. I grieve the loss of time as well as my husband. I did not know that you can grieve the loss of time, but I do. I have watched my life go by for fifteen years, and now I struggle to say goodbye and I struggle to say hello.

Ignore people who tell you, "I know how you feel." I know how I felt. I can't and will never tell you, "I know how YOU feel." I do not know how YOU feel, and I never will. I do not know you. I did not know your loved one. I do not know anything about your relationship with them or with life in general. The biggest thing happening in your life is not the biggest thing happening in my life. I can only tell you what I felt and how I feel now.

There were times I thought my heart could not bear so much pain and it would give in. I still feel my husband's heart in the palm of my hand. His last heartbeat was so easy…just a beat…silence. I felt my own mortality in that moment. The world did not tremble, the clock on the wall did not stop, an angel did not come, a beam of light did not brighten the room, no music fled the air…just a beat…silence…while the ignorant clock on the wall kept ticking and the bird outside kept chiming. The world did not stop because I fought to stay standing in caregiver shoes for fifteen years. The world did not end because my husband died.

I do not have all the answers. I will not tell you that the journey is easy. You might feel like you are riding an emotional roller-coaster, or hanging from a tree with your head down, or drowning. There are no shortcuts, there are no tricks, there is no magic. There is no road map, and you can't follow someone else's path; you will have to make every step of the way on your own. Breathe and follow whatever makes you feel better, more alive, happy. Your life is not going to start when the pain goes away. The pain will become bearable and unbearable part of you when you start your life. You will not get better or feel better. You will learn to cope. At least, that is happening to me.

You are at the end of the journey. You have stopped. Pause…turn around…look. Close the books; let another journey begin…Step 1

APPENDIX
WHAT DO YOU SEE?

- ?
- ?
- ?

What do you want to see?

- ?
- ?
- ?

Now, what do you going to do about it? You still have the time.

- ?
- ?
- ?